LOVE LESSONS

FACING PAGES | **FACING PAGES**

NICHOLAS JENKINS

Series Editor

After Every War: Twentieth-Century Women Poets
translations from the German by Eavan Boland

Horace, the Odes: New Translations by Contemporary Poets
edited by J. D. McClatchy

Hothouses: Poems 1889
by Maurice Maeterlinck
translated by Richard Howard

Landscape with Rowers: Poetry from the Netherlands
translated and introduced by J. M. Coetzee

The Night
by Jaime Saenz
translated and introduced by Forrest Gander and Kent Johnston

Love Lessons: Selected Poems of Alda Merini
translated by Susan Stewart

Love Lessons

Selected Poems of Alda Merini

Translated by Susan Stewart

PRINCETON UNIVERSITY PRESS

PRINCETON AND OXFORD

Copyright © 2009 by Princeton University Press
Published by Princeton University Press, 41 William Street,
    Princeton, New Jersey 08540
In the United Kingdom: Princeton University Press, 6 Oxford Street,
    Woodstock, Oxfordshire OX20 1TW

All Rights Reserved

LIBRARY OF CONGRESS CATALOGING-IN-PUBLICATION DATA
Merini, Alda, 1931–
    [Poems. English & Italian. Selections]
    Love lessons : selected poems of Alda Merini / translated by Susan Stewart.
        p.   cm. — (Facing pages)
    Includes bibliographical references.
    ISBN 978-0-691-12938-9 (alk. paper)
    I. Stewart, Susan (Susan A.), 1952– II. Title.
    PQ4829.E57A2 2009
    851'.91—dc22   2008021695

British Library Cataloging-in-Publication Data is available

This book has been composed in Stempel Garamond and Diotima

Printed on acid-free paper. ∞

press.princeton.edu

10 9 8 7 6 5 4 3 2 1

Contents

Acknowledgments

Alda Merini's poems have been translated with her permission and the permission of her publisher, Einaudi. I am grateful to Ambrogio Borsani for his help with that process and for making it possible for me to meet Merini in Milano in January 2006.

The support and enthusiasm of Nicholas Jenkins, the series editor, and Hanne Winarsky, at Princeton University Press, have eased my work from the beginning.

Luca Grillo reviewed, with his native Milanese eye, every word of this translation; I could not have completed it without him, though any weaknesses here remain my own.

This translation is dedicated to Brunella Antomarini, who urged me to undertake the project and commented on many of its pages; to Pia Candinas, who first gave me a book of Merini's writing; and to Maria Cristina Biggio, who has done so much to further the life of American poetry in Italy — their devotion to the culture and poetry of all languages is an inspiration.

Translator's Introduction

> I tenderly loved some very sweet lovers
> without them knowing anything about it.
> And I wove spiderwebs from this
> and I always fell prey to my own creation.
> In me there was the soul of the prostitute
> of the saint of the one who lusts for blood and of the hypocrite.
> Many people gave a label to my way of life
> and all that while I was only an hysteric.
>
> —"Alda Merini"

Alda Merini's front door stands at the top of several flights of stairs in a nineteenth-century building along the canal in the Naviglio district of Milano. Posted there, a card displays a sad poetic tribute to her publisher Vanni Scheiwiller: *Un uomo che volò alto / talmente alto / che molti indeboliti spiriti / l'atterrarono* (*A man who flew high / so high / that many weaker spirits / brought him down*). Inside, dusky sunlight pours in from the shuttered windows of the three rooms that make up her small apartment—kitchen, bath, and bedroom strung along a hallway. Within this warren, Merini has assembled, on every available surface, a chaotic, indecipherable archive of her existence: pages and objects and remnants stacked, dropped, leaning, falling, rising toward the ceiling, spilling over the floors and across tables, into her bed, across bureaus and shelves. Tottering boxes, books, reams of paper and loose sheets, magazines, parts of magazines, cast-off clothing, discarded bouquets and bills, jars and bottles—implements, so many imaginable, unimaginable things. Visitors

1

enter, stepping where they can, steadying themselves, sitting a while to talk, the phone ringing, the CD player on pause, the door open to the hallway where, eventually, after conversation and perhaps an improvised poem or two, they will go out again—Merini's privacy an ongoing open secret.

Across the ochre palimpsest of peeling paint above her bed, in lurid lines of lipsticks and faint pencil traces, she has scrawled a vast map of phone numbers, aphorisms, fragments of poems coming to life or fading from memory; it's hard to tell. She roams, a small stooped figure, through her realm of objects, dropping cigarette ash everywhere she goes. If you do not believe in guardian angels, the sight of Alda Merini orbiting through this flammable maze, day after day, night after night, shedding sparks, might make you change your mind.

Is this space, organized so that everything is ready to hand as material for art, with nothing left to insignificance or mere appearance, the house of a madwoman? Is it not bourgeois life, with its discrete material categories of things and persons, that indicates an obstinate insanity? Who, after all, would complain about the housekeeping of the Cumaean Sibyl? As Merini writes in "When the Anguish":

> And, up against me, the inanimate things
> that I created earlier
> come to die again within the breast
> of my intelligence
> eager for my shelter and my fruits,
> begging again for riches from a beggar.

Such conscientious care for debris, such obliviousness toward any existing system of value, gives evidence of the daily poetic needs of choosing, making, and judging anew from the manifold of phenomena that surround us. There is no alienation in Merini's environment—only memory, imagination, and an innovative, unending hospitality toward poetry and persons, a state of vigilant reception. Meanwhile, the life and work are not in hiding; they wait in plain sight.

The biography of Alda Merini is well known to Italian readers through her many interviews and the introductions to her books. Yet there is as yet no full scholarly biography, and what we know of her life comes largely from her own words. Born in Milano on the first day of Spring, 1931, she was one of four children, three of whom survived into adulthood. Her mother, a housewife, was the daughter of a schoolteacher from Lodi, but the mother nevertheless discouraged Alda's desire for a classical education. In contrast, her father, a clerk for a national insurance company—the Assicurazioni Generali of Venezia—encouraged her literary aspirations from an early age, giving her spelling lessons and books. She frequently recounts how she read a book of art history and Dante's *Commedia* at the age of eight, and memorized many of Dante's passages. A sickly child, she often didn't go to school, but her father continued to give her exercises in reading and writing, and a teacher came regularly to give her piano lessons.

As she approached adolescence, Merini had an intense desire to become a nun, but her mother objected to this plan, too, contending the girl was better suited to having a family. This period of disappointment for the young Merini intersected with the height of Italy's involvement in World War II. Merini has recorded that her father was not a member of the fascist party, and during the 1942 bombardment of Milan the family fled to the nearby town of Trecate in search of food and safety. There Merini had no piano to play, but she remembered this time as one of solidarity with other refugees. When the family returned to Milano at the end of the war, they found their house severely damaged. They broke it up into apartments to be let out to strangers, for the father had no source of income, and Merini herself was sent to a vocational school where she studied stenography in preparation for finding work in an office.

Her father had published a little pamphlet of her poems when she was ten. At fifteen she was dedicating herself to writing poems and, at the same time, suffering from severe anorexia, a condition exacerbated by memories of wartime deprivation. She was sent to stay with an uncle in Torino while she was treated by a well-known neurologist there. When she returned to Milano, she did find a post as a stenographer and held it for a brief time. Meanwhile, by the age of sixteen, she was writing more mature poems. In 1947 some of these poems came to the attention of Silvana Rovelli, a cousin of the well-known poet Ada Negri. Rovelli mentioned Merini's poems to the writer Angelo Romanò, who in turn showed them to the influential critic and anthologist Giacinto Spagnoletti.

Rovelli's intervention made a dramatic difference in the life of the young Merini. Later in that year, she started to go often to Spagnoletti's house, where she found a remarkable salon attended by many of the period's most prominent poets and critics—Giorgio Manganelli, Pier Paolo Pasolini, Maria Corti, and Luciano Erba, among others. The teenaged girl became a kind of mascot for the group and at sixteen she began a love affair with Manganelli, who, at twenty-seven, already had a wife and children. In 1947, too, her first symptoms of serious mental illness began and she spent a month at the Villa Turro clinic in Milano. The affair with Manganelli lasted until 1949, when he left both Merini and his family for Rome.

In 1950 Spagnoletti published two of the nineteen-year-old Merini's poems, works she had written several years before, in his anthology *Poesia italiana contemporanea 1909–1949.* The next year a group of her lyrics was published, at the suggestion of Eugenio Montale, in another important anthology, Vanni Scheiwiller's edition of women poets, *Poetesse del Novocento.* Even in these earliest lyrics, we find Merini's enduring emphases upon chiaroscuro lighting, eroticism, and mysticism. Between 1950 and 1953 she became romantically involved with another member of the Spagnoletti group, Salvatore Quasimodo, who was thirty years her senior.

When this affair ended in 1953, she married Ettore Carniti, the owner of a chain of bakery-pastry shops in Milano—a man with no particular background in literature and culture. Even so, Merini's career as a poet continued to grow. Her first book, *La presenza di Orfeo,* was published in that year. In a 1954 essay in the important cultural journal *Paragone,* Pier Paolo Pasolini wrote of her as a "young Milanese girl" who already was showing the influence of Campana, Rilke, George, and Trakl—he intuitively grasped the importance her often troubled psychology would have in her work. At the same time, he marveled at how a young poet could have absorbed such intense and monumental influences. Scheiwiller also continued to champion Merini's poems, publishing in 1955 a collection titled *Paura di Dio* that included all her poems from 1947 to 1953. And 1955 saw the publication of her *Nozze romane* by the publishing house Schwarz—in this book, reflecting on her early married life, she continues to be influenced strongly by Rilke's imagery and voice, a textual encounter she often cites in interviews as her entry into a visionary poetry.

Merini's first daughter, Emanuela (Manuela), was also born in 1955. The baby was cared for by a young Sicilian pediatrician, Pietro di Pasquale, and he became an unre-quited love interest—sadly, the first of many—for Merini. She named her next book *Tu sei Pietro*, dedicating the poem "Genesi" to the doctor while also exploring the religious im-agery associated with the disciple Peter. Scheiwiller pub-lished this book in 1961, though most of the poems were written in 1955.

And then, between 1955 and 1975—with her second daughter, Flavia, born in 1958—Merini fell silent. For much of this time, she was kept in mental institutions where she suffered frequent isolation, the imposition of physical re-straints, and more than thirty-seven electrical shock treat-ments. Initially committed by her husband, Carniti, she en-tered the Paolo Pini asylum in Milano in 1965 and remained there until 1972. During relatively brief periods with her family during these years, she gave birth to two more daugh-ters, Barbara and Simona, though she was not well enough to raise them. The periods of madness continued until she began writing again in the mid-1970s.

Ettore Carniti died in 1981 and that year, at the age of fifty, Merini began a correspondence with the poet and doc-tor Michele Pierri, who was then eighty-two years old. By 1983 she had married him and moved to his home in Taranto, in the southern region of Puglia, but she became seriously mentally ill once more and went into an oppressive Taran-tese mental institution. The poems of *La Terra Santa*, an ac-count of her illness during this period, were first published in 1982 in journals. She couldn't find a publisher, but then Vanni Scheiwiller again supported her, bringing out the book in 1984. In 1993 *La Terra Santa* received the prestigious na-tional Montale Prize, thus symbolically completing the cir-cle of Montale's own support for her early work.

Leaving Taranto, Merini returned to Milano in 1986,

where she was treated by the psychiatrist Marcella Rizzo and finally was able to live outside of mental institutions in her own apartment, that space I have earlier described. Since her return to the Naviglio, Merini has published a book of poems or prose almost annually. Her autobiographical writings—*L'altra verità: diario d'una diversa* of 1987, *Delirio amoroso* of 1989, and *Reato di vita* of 1994 recount her years of incarceration in asylums, always in an intensely phenomenological and aphoristic style. With the death of Manganelli, her early love and mentor, in 1991, she published, between 1992 and 1996, a virtual explosion of new poems: *Ipotenusa d'amore*; *La Palude di Manganelli, o il monarca del re*; and *Un'anima indocile*. Her *Titano amori interno* of 1993 introduced a new, more colloquial, and open style, one that continued in her two books of 1995: *La pazza della porta accanta* and *Ballate non pagate*. Merini's work up until this point won her the prestigious Premio Viareggio in 1996 and simultaneously she was nominated by the French Academy for the Nobel Prize.

The critic Maria Corti—who had known Merini from her earliest teenaged visits to Spagnoletti's salon and had provided crucial help as she emerged from her illness to write *La Terra Santa* more than a decade earlier—assembled in 1997 the most important selection of her work, *Fiore di poesia*. The collection won the 1997 Premio Procida-Elsa Morante and, in 1999, the Italian government's Premio della Presidenza del consiglio dei Ministri, settore Poesia. In this period Merini also brought out two new books, *Aforismi e magie* and *Vuoto d'amore*. A collection of brief lyrics, *Superba è la Notte*, appeared in 2000. In 2001 the Italian PEN Club made her their candidate for the Nobel Prize. New poems, *Alla tua salute, amore mio: poesie, aforismi*, and a memoir, *Clinica Dell'Abbandono*, were published in 2003, and in 2005 she produced another pair of memoirs and poems: *Uomini miei* and *Sono nata il ventuno a primavera: Diario e nuove poesie.*

Reading Merini reveals that her lyrics and meditative poems are characterized by a number of distinctive techniques. Much of their immediacy arises from her use of what might be called "then / now" structures that resemble the dynamic between confession and prayer. In poems like "[As for me, I used to be a bird]" and "[There was a fountain that offered dawns]," as well as the more directly imploring "Antique Lyric" and her apostrophe to her daughter "[Stay steady burning olive tree]," she creates a strong sense of presence that arises from the request made by the speaking voice. Beggars, outstretched palms, and the saints who help them are frequent figures in her work. Merini's narratives, often broken by the unsaid via the use of ellipses, similarly confront the reader with the urgency of a demand—the "when / then / now" dynamic of these poems effects a turning in time that comes hurtling out of the past toward the present moment of encounter.

In other work, especially in her early poems, her use of the future tense or her setting out of hypothetical cases invites the reader, in contrast, to enter into a reflective process of judgment. There is a vatic tone in the poems, only underlined by her practice of writing aphorisms and her unusual use of dramatic monologue in her poem on the Cumaean Sibyl herself.

If these are some dominant aspects of Merini's use of time and personal history, the space of her work is a space of bodily memory placed within the larger sphere of the city of Milano. Parts of the body recur here so frequently as poetic subjects that they have some of the disembodied power of sacred relics: hands, faces, mouths, wombs, loins, teeth, the pupils of the eye, lips, breasts, throats, eyelashes, voices, big toes, fingernails, testicles, feet, napes, hair, skin. The body is revealed as a place of suffering and joy, a shelter for the reason and the emotions at once. In the poems of *Superba è la Notte*, especially the long meditations entitled "The Raven" and "Cry of Death," somatic experience anchors the surrealistic play of metaphysical topics.

Merini's syntax is something like a nervous system in itself. Whatever regularity stems from her reliance on a basic five-beat line is countered by her use of enjambment, seemingly arbitrary punctuation, and surprising, complex, phrase and sentence structures. From the inverted syntax—with prepositions and verbs preceding their subjects—in the early "Mary of Egypt" to the winding clauses of the late long poems, Merini often torques the syntax and "lands" on either a clear, and separate, final couplet or on passages that return the ear to earlier language. For example, "[Naviglio that succors my flesh]" ends with a kind of fireworks display of recurring sounds :

> . . . Incorniciata
> la fronte di frescure inusitate
> batto i denti nel freddo meridiano
> dove adagio si stendono le suore.

The unusual end rhymes of "Othello," with its one strong unrhymed line, can be compared to the juxtaposition in "[What unbearable chiaroscuro]" of *aaaa* end-rhyming in the first stanza and no end-rhymes in the second stanza. At the same time, the insistent initial end-rhymes find their counterpart in the flat repetition of the second stanza's *perché / perché / perché*, each beginning one of the stanza's three sentences.

This resonant repetition of "Why?" speaks to two incompatible, yet also strangely resonant, myths that have, since the beginning, animated much of Merini's work. The first is the ancient Greek myth of Orpheus and Eurydice, the story of the bereaved husband / poet who went to Hades to plea for the return of his dead wife and could succeed only on the condition that he not turn around to look at her as they ascended back to the daylit world—a condition Orpheus could not meet. The second is the Christian myth of Peter, the apostle and founder of the Church who pledged his fidelity to his Lord at the time of the Crucifixion, but, as Christ predicted, denied that fidelity three times before the cock crowed at the dawn of the next day. These myths tell the same story: as Merini puts it in her poem "Sappho," they result in "the most dismaying dazzling / of an unfairly denied love." Such love, risked and fulfilled, is betrayed. And that betrayal, which is simultaneously an abandonment, leads on to the fulfillment of a true vocation: in the first case, the vocation of the poet, in the second, that of the patriarch.

Hearing the account of Eurydice's two deaths—that insistent, more-than-traumatic repetition—we can surmise it was not out of mere carelessness that Orpheus turned to doom her. Master poet and yet husband of insufficient commitment, Orpheus is, for Merini, a figure of "unbearable chiaroscuro," an irresolvable ambivalence. As we say, though it goes without saying, the woman poet cannot "identify" with him.

If such a minimal condition of recognition cannot be met, the loss nevertheless is not great, for ideas of identification are, in the end, banal. Nor is it necessary for the woman poet, neglected by Orpheus, to identify with his twice-sacrificed lover. It is true that Merini's poems are replete with examples of the turned gaze, where a slighting attention brings destruction, where mere curiosity freezes person to thing—and she, Alda Merini, the living poet, is the object of that gaze. That, however, is the beginning, not the end, of such predicaments, for Merini emerges speaking, and she emerges speaking with a body, as she proclaims in the closing of her early poem "The Presence of Orpheus":

So, within your shaping arms
I pour myself, small and immense,
serene given, restless given,
unending developing motion.

Here Eurydice neither disappears nor "remains." She finds she can sing, and Orpheus is not her only subject. Let's substitute a better, more truthful banality: as soon as one is no longer a testifying victim, one begins to be a speaking person. Love, like war and poetry, is made by declaration; despite their incommensurable means, they each can only commence in speech and speech is, too, their aftermath.

It is the foundational continuity of voice that also is both source and outcome of Merini's own Orphism, an aesthetic she was determined to develop out of a hermetic tradition that continually and paradoxically both underscored and overlooked the sacrifice of Eurydice. Initially conforming to these "measures," pouring herself literally, most often erotically, into the mold of those male poets who were her mentors and then abandoned her, she discovers, in the course of her long career, a range of thinking and creating that makes out of the aphoristic and discursive, the occasional and the eternal, one continuous work.

When we take up the story of the disciple Peter, we find another account of love's recognition and betrayal, one told with slight variations throughout the four Gospels. At Matthew 17:18–20, Christ blesses Simon Bar-jona, the fisherman, under his new identity as the disciple Peter, telling him "thou art Peter, and upon this rock I will build my church," thereby declaring to him the meaning of his name as rock. At the same time, Christ delivers the following interdiction to Peter and all the disciples: "They should tell no man that he was Jesus the Christ." As the moment of the Crucifixion approaches, Christ tells Peter, despite his protestations, "before the cock crows, thou shalt deny me thrice." Once Christ is taken, all the disciples flee except Peter, who remains in the high priest's palace; when Christ then is condemned to death, two young women come toward Peter and accuse him of being a follower of Jesus. At the first accusation, Peter says "I know not what thou sayest" (Matthew 26:18). At the second, he says, with an oath, "I do not know the man" (26:72). And then, as other bystanders say he has, by his dialect as a Galilean (Mark 14:70), betrayed his status as a follower of Jesus of Nazareth, Peter curses and swears in response, saying "I know not the man." (Matthew 26:74) or "I know not this man of whom ye speak" (Mark 15:71). At that, the cock crows, and Peter, recognizing Christ's prediction has come to pass, weeps bitterly.

Naming, speaking, denying, prophesying, incomprehension, familiarity, dialect, referentiality—the story of Peter is a strange amalgam of failed and successful, intended and unconscious, speech acts determining affiliation. The story presents a classic case of the kind of double-binding interdiction that produces schizophrenia: do this and don't do this—speak my name as a rock that cannot speak. It also is a classic case of a gnomic prediction—you will deny me (and hence obey this prophecy). For Merini, Peter's betrayal becomes emblematic of all relations where one figure loves unequivocally and out of balance with his or her object: the asymmetry of passionate love; the asymmetry of family obligation; the asymmetry of love between mother and child. She declares in "And it would be even easier":

As for my crying over you, I bleached it away slowly
day by day as full light does
and in silence I sent it back to my eyes,
which, if I look at you, are alive with stars.

Such uneven or non-existent reciprocity is the necessary
condition of a founding love that precedes any notion of
economy and must resist the contingency of errors and fail-
ures of communication.

This account brings us to the present translation, which is
made up of selections from *Fiore di poesia*, hence all of Me-
rini's books up until 1997, including the aphorisms that first
appeared in that volume, and other lyrics from the 2000 col-
lection, *Superba è la notte*. My title, *Love Lessons* (*Lezioni
d'amore*), was suggested by Merini herself when she viewed
the completed translation in November 2007.

In her *Delirio amoroso*, Merini wrote, ambiguously, "All
my books are tied to my mental illness, almost always
wanted by others to witness my damnation," thereby not
indicating whether it is her books or the mental illness itself,
or their inter-relation, that was demanded by her audience.
Indeed her tremendous, bestselling popularity in Italy—wit-
nessed by the fact that her books can be found in the kiosks
of every Italian train station as well as every bookstore—
speaks to the importance of the Merini legend of the mad
poet. If you find yourself in a conversation with the Italian,
mostly male, poets of her generation, a mention of Merini's
name will quickly bring out somewhat sullen condemna-
tions of her "sensationalism" and ostensibly undeserved rec-
ognition by "feminists" and others. And if you speak to
feminists about her, you will find that they complain about
her subservience to male mentors or her irrational imagery.

As she was once the mascot of older male poets, she is now too often the mascot of younger fans who admire her less for her poetry than her persona. Merini thereby continues to be both honored and dismissed by acknowledgments of her gifts as a poet, gifts that truly cannot be explained away. Yet in everything she has written, the terrible facts of the twentieth century, and her experience of them, loom; she is both learned in the tradition and schooled in suffering—to deny either aspect of her experience is not to read her at all.

Poetry, at least since Callimachus and Ovid, has been concerned deeply with the aetiology of things both ordinary and extraordinary, and in Merini's obsessions and successes at once we can see a mind uncovering, inferring causes, seeking out lessons to be learned—even traumatic ones—within a larger practice of poetry as a steady means of discovery. Consider the progress of one of her most perfect lyrics:

> As for me, I used to be a bird
> with a gentle white womb,
> someone cut my throat
>   just for laughs,
>   I don't know.
> As for me, I used to be a great albatross
> and whirled over the seas.
> Someone put an end to my journey,
> without any charity in the tone of it.
> But even stretched out on the ground
> I sing for you now
> my songs of love.

The Villa Fiorita mental hospital, the western ring-road, the Naviglio district, Lombardian sinners—all anchor the poems in Milano's public reality. Meanwhile, her natural images—the moon, the grass, asphodels and violets, fruit, an olive tree, snow, a raven, even a crocodile—tend toward universal significance, accompanying a mental world of paradises, saints and angels who coexist with the literature and myths of pagan antiquity.

Like her American peers Sylvia Plath and Anne Sexton— all born within just a few years of each other—understanding her own mental states, and their origin in historical and psychological events, has been key to her outlook as a poet. But unlike the work of Plath, Sexton, and other poets of the Anglo-American confessional school, Merini's poetry always has had a metaphysical frame and she continually places her experience within these larger patterns of history and myth. Perhaps in the end this broader palette, this more profound sense of her place in the world, has enabled her to save her own life.

Roma
October 2007

from *Fiore di Poesia: 1951–1997*

La presenza di Orfeo

a Giorgio Manganelli

Non ti preparerò col mio mostrarmiti
ad una confidenza limitata,
ma perché nel toccarmi la tua mano
non abbia una memoria di presagi,
giacerò nell'informe
fusa io stessa, sciolta dentro il buio,
per quanto possa, elaborata e viva,
ridivenire caos . . .

Orfeo novello amico dell'assenza,
modulerai di nuovo dalla cetra
la figura nascente di me stessa.
Sarai alle soglie piano e divinante
di un mistero assoluto di silenzio,
ignorando i miei limiti di un tempo,
godrai il possesso della sola essenza.

Allora, concretandomi in un primo
accenno di presenza,
sarò un ramo fiorito di consenso,
e poi, trovato un punto di contatto,
ammetterò una timida coscienza
di vita d'animale
e mi dirò che non andrò piú oltre,
mentre già mi sviluppi,
sapienza ineluttabile e sicura,
in un gioco insperato di armonie,
in una conclusione di fanciulla . . .

THE PRESENCE OF ORPHEUS

for Giorgio Manganelli

I won't prepare you by revealing myself to you
in a bound-about closeness,
but just in case your hand, in touching me,
might hold a memory of omens,
I'll lie down, fused
with what is formless, melted within the darkness,
as far as I can, secreted and alive,
becoming chaos again . . .

Orpheus, new friend of absence,
out of your lyre you'll tune once more
my dawning figure.
At the threshold, you'll be gentle, divining
silence's absolute mystery,
unaware of my limits from so long ago,
you'll leap for joy, holding the lonely essence.

Then, steeling myself in a first
hint of presence,
I'll be an unfolding flower of consent
and then, finding a point of contact,
I'll let in a timid conscience
of animal life
and I'll tell myself that I won't keep trying
so long as you're already shaping me,
ineluctable and certain wisdom,
into an unhoped-for game of harmonies
all the way to a girlish conclusion.

Fanciulla: è questo il termine raggiunto?
E per l'addietro non l'ho maturato
e non l'ho poi distrutto
delusa, offesa in ogni volontà?
Che vuol dire fanciulla
se non superamento di coscienza?
Era questo di me che non volevo:
condurmi, trascurando ogni mia forma,
al vertice mortale della vita . . .
Ma la presenza d'ogni mia sembianza
quale urgenza incalzante di sviluppo,
quale presto proporsi
e piú presto risolversi d'enigmi!

E quando poi, dal mio aderire stesso,
la forma scivolò in un altro tempo
di piú rare e piú estranee conclusioni,
quando del mio "sentirmi" voluttuoso
rimane un'aderenza di dolore,
allora, allora preferii la morte
che ribadisse in me questo possesso.

Ma ci si può avanzare nella vita
mano che regge e fiaccola portata
e ci si può liberamente dare
alle dimenticanze piú serene
quando gli anelli multipli di noi
si sciolgono e riprendono in accordo,
quando la garanzia dell'immanenza
ci fasci di un benessere assoluto.

Girl: is this the end point?
Didn't I reach it long ago
and then didn't I destroy it
disappointed, offended by my own willfulness?
What does girl mean
other than an overcoming of conscience?
It was exactly what I didn't want for myself:
leading me, neglecting all my form,
to life's mortal climax . . .
But the presence of every one of my appearances
what urgent urging of growth,
what quick offering
and quicker solution to mysteries!

And when, from my very same touch,
the form slipped into another time
of rarer and stranger endings,
when, of all my voluptuous "feelings,"
only an attachment to suffering remains,
then, then I preferred death,
which nails down that possession within me.

But someone can go ahead in life
hand that holds and bears the torch
and someone can freely give in
to the most serene forgetting
when the many rings of ourselves
are melted down and retrieved in turn,
when the promise of immanence
wraps around us with an absolute well-being.

Cosí, nelle tue braccia ordinatrici
io mi riverso, minima ed immensa;
dato sereno, dato irrefrenabile,
attività perenne di sviluppo.

So, within your shaping arms
I pour myself, small and immense,
serene given, restless given,
unending developing motion.

SARÒ SOLA?

Quando avrò alzato in me l'intimo fuoco
che originava già queste bufere
e sarò salda, libera, vitale,
allora sarò sola?

E forse staccherò dalle radici
la rimossa speranza dell'amore,
ricorderò che frutto d'ogni
limite umano è assenza di memoria,
tutta mi affonderò nel divenire . . .

Ma fino a che io tremo del principio
cui la tua mano mi iniziò da ieri,
ogni attributo vivo che mi preme
giace incomposto nelle tue misure.

Will I Be Alone?

When, within me, the intimate fire awakens
that was the source of these storms
and I am steady, free, alive,
then will I be alone?

And maybe I will rip out by the roots
my postponed hope for love,
I will remember that the fruit of every
human limit is memory's absence,
which plunges me into becoming . . .

But until I shiver from the touch
of your hand, since yesterday my initiation,
every sign of life that presses me
lies unshaped within your fixed measures.

SOLO UNA MANO D'ANGELO

Solo una mano d'angelo
intatta di sé, del suo amore per sé,
potrebbe
offrirmi la concavità del suo palmo
perché vi riversi il mio pianto.
La mano dell'uomo vivente
è troppo impiagliata nei fili dell'oggi e dell'ieri,
è troppo ricolma di vita e di plasma di vita!
Non potrà mai la mano dell'uomo mondarsi
per il tranquillo pianto del proprio fratello!
E dunque, soltanto una mano di angelo bianco
dalle lontane radici nutrite d'eterno e d'immenso
potrebbe filtrare serena le confessioni dell'uomo
senza vibrarne sul fondo in un cenno di viva ripulsa.

ONLY AN ANGEL'S HAND

Only an angel's hand
unsullied in itself, in its love for itself,
could
offer me the hollow of its palm
reversing my crying into it.
The hand of a living man
is too tangled in the threads of todays and yesterdays,
is too filled with life and the living plasma of life!
A man's hand will never cleanse itself
on behalf of his own brother's calm crying
And so, only a white angel's hand
out of distant roots, nourished by eternity and
        immensity,
could calmly sift man's confessions
without shaking at the palm in a sign of intense
        repulsion.

Maria Egiziaca

(Tintoretto)

Sulla chiara aderenza del suo viso
dove balena il ritmico, selvaggio,
sentimento dell'alba
mentre della notturna s'addolora
quiete silvestre e cinge a dominare
il boato del tempo la più cauta
trepida luce, salgono veloci
i profili irrequieti del destino.

Mirabile linguaggio che trascorre
dalle limpide acque alla vibrata
forza dell'inumana profezia!

. . . .

Ora nell'ampia conca dell'eremo
un soffuso candore si raccoglie
dalle acque sui rami ed accompagna
di cenni lacrimevoli il congedo.

MARY OF EGYPT

(Tintoretto)

On her face's clear adherence
flashes dawn's rhythmic
wild perception,
mourns the night's
sylvan stillness and
overcomes encircles
the noise of time the most careful
trembling light, quickly arise
destiny's restless profiles.

Marvelous language that runs
from pure waters to the vibrant
strength of inhuman prophecy!

. . . .

Now in the open palm of the hermit
a suffused brightness is gathered
from the dew on the branches and it lights up
tearful farewells, gestures of goodbye.

PAX

Leva morte da noi
quell'intatto minuto come pane
che l'amante non morse né la donna
al colmo dell'offerta.
Dove vita, di sé fatta piú piena
ci divide dal corpo
e ci annovera al gregge di un Pastore
costruito di luce,
nasce morte per te. D'ogni dolore
parto ultimo e solo
che mai possa procedere dal seno . . .
Eppure a noi lontano desiderio
di quell'attimo pieno
viene a fatica dentro giorni oscuri
ma se calasse nella perfezione
di sua vera natura
presto cadremmo affranti dalla luce.
L'albero non è albero né il fiore
può decidersi bello
quando sia forte l'anima di male;
ma nel giorno di morte
quando l'amante, tenebroso duce
abbandona le redini del sangue,
sí, piú pura vicenda
si spiegherà entro un ordine di regno.
Ed il senso verrà ricostruito,
e ogni cosa nel letto
in cui cadde nel tempo avrà respiro,

PEACE

Death take away from us
that untouched minute like bread
that the lover didn't bite into, nor the woman
at the climax of the offering.
Where life, brimming over with itself,
divides us from our bodies
and numbers us among the flock of a Shepherd
built of light,
death is born for you. Out of every suffering
the ultimate and only birth
that might ever proceed from the womb . . .
Even so, to us a far desire
of that brimming instant
comes struggling inside dark days
though if it plunged into the perfection
of its true essence
soon we would fall, devastated by the light.
The tree is not a tree and the flower
cannot decide on its own to be beautiful
when evil's soul might be strengthened.
But at the day of death
when the lover, the shadowy charioteer,
lets go of the bloody reins,
yes, a purer episode
will unfold itself within a rule of the realm.
And the meaning will be revealed,
and everything in the bed
where everything fell will breathe in time,

un respiro perfetto.
Ora solo un impuro desiderio
può rimuovere tutto, ma domani
quando morte s'innalzi . . .

a perfect breath.
Now only an impure desire
can take away everything, but tomorrow
when death still might rise up . . .

NOZZE ROMANE

Sí, questa sarà la nostra casa,
oggi arrivo a capirlo;
ma tu, uomo gaudente, chi sei?
Ti misuro: una formula eterna.
Hai assunto un aspetto inesorabile.

Mi scaverai fin dove ho le radici
(non per cercarmi, non per aiutarmi)
tutto scoperchierai che fu nascosto
per la ferocia di malsane usanze.

Avrai in potere le mie fondamenta
uomo che mi costringi;
ferirai le mie carni col tuo dente,
t'insedierai al fervore d'un anelito
per soffocarne il senso dell'urgenza.

Come una pietra che divide un corso,
un corso d'acqua giovane e irruente,
tu mi dividerai con incoscienza
nelle braccia di un delta doloroso . . .

ROMAN WEDDING

Yes, this will be our house,
today I'm here to see it;
but you, lusty man, who are you?
I take your measure: an eternal formula.
You take on an inexorable look.

You will dig me down to my roots
(not to search for me, not to help me)
you will strip away everything hidden
through the savagery of your crazy habits.

You will overpower my core
man who forces me:
you will wound my flesh with your teeth,
you will settle into the fervor of my yearning
to choke its sense of urgency.

Like a rock dividing waters,
a young and raging current,
recklessly, you will break me up
in the arms of a painful delta . . .

La Pietà

Ora si piega la visione acuta
delle cose superne
sopra il linguaggio oscuro di un presente
pienamente scontato. All'improvviso
vuoto è fatto nel grembo già maturo
di letizia inumana. In un profluvio
d'ipotetico pianto si insapora,
velame spento di una forza antica
poggiata sopra il fremito piú basso
d'un fuoco, in forza del divino, vivo.
E cosí Morte inizia la sua insidia
con un violento grido circolare.

The Pietà

Now the acute vision
of supreme things bends
over the hidden language
of a fully atoned present. Improvising
in the already mature womb
of inhuman delight. In a profusion
of hypothetical crying it's seasoned,
the spent veil of an ancient force,
leaning on the fire's lowest
quiver, with divine force, alive.
And so Death begins its ambush
with a violent circling cry.

La Sibilla Cumana

Ho veduto virgulti
spegnersi a un sommo d'intima dolcezza
quasi per ridondanza di messaggi
e disciogliersi labbra
a lungo stemperate nella voce,
nell'urlo, quasi, della propria vita;
vuota di sé ho scrutata la pupilla,
impoverito il trepido magnete
che attirava in delirio le figure.
Cosí, sopra una forma già distesa
nel certo abbraccio dell'intuizione,
crolla la lenta pausa finale
che intossica di morte l'avventura.

THE CUMAEAN SIBYL

I saw blossoms
fade away at the peak of intimate tenderness
maybe because the messages were redundant
and lips melting
for a long time slurred in the voice,
in the cry, maybe, of their own life;
I scrutinized the pupil of the eye, emptied of itself,
the trembling magnet, impoverished,
that drew the figures in frenzy.
This is how, above a form, already outstretched
in intuition's sure embrace,
the slow final interval gives way,
poisoning the adventure with death.

QUANDO L'ANGOSCIA

Quando l'angoscia spande il suo colore
dentro l'anima buia
come una pennellata di vendetta,
sento il germoglio dell'antica fame
farsi timido e grigio
e morire la luce del domani.

E contro me le cose inanimate
che ho creato dapprima
vengono a rimorire dentro il seno
della mia intelligenza
avide del mio asilo e dei miei frutti,
richiedenti ricchezza ad un mendíco.

WHEN THE ANGUISH

When the anguish spreads its color
inside the dark soul
like revenge's brushstroke,
I feel the budding shoot of an ancient hunger
becoming shy and gray
and the light of tomorrow dying.

And, up against me, the inanimate things
that I created earlier
come to die again within the breast
of my intelligence
eager for my shelter and my fruits,
begging again for riches from a beggar.

Missione di Pietro

Quando il Signore, desolato e grigio,
ombra della Sua ombra incespicava
dentro il Suo verbo colmo di incertezza,
Pietro comparve, forte nelle braccia
e nelle membra a reggerLo nel mondo . . .

Quando Pietro fu solo nel peccato,
quando già rinnegava il Suo Signore
e Lo vendeva a tutti nella frode,
Dio non comparve (si era già velato
per la notte piú oscura profetata),
ma gli fece suonare dentro il cuore
le campane piú vive del riscatto.

PIETRO FU IL PRIMO A IMMERGERSI NEL SANGUE!

Peter's Mission

When the Lord, desolate and gray,
shadow of His shadows, was stumbling
inside His own Word, and filled with uncertainty,
Peter showed up, strong-armed,
strong in every limb, to carry Him into the world . . .

When Peter was left alone in his own sin,
when he was already denying His Lord
and was selling Him to everyone, a bait and switch,
God didn't show up (He had already veiled himself
for the darkest prophesied night),
but he let ring inside his heart
the most vivid bells of ransom.

PETER WAS THE FIRST TO DIVE INTO BLOOD!

SOGNO

Lungo il tempo infinito della Grecia
quando concesso era il paradiso
alle fanciulle in tèpidi giardini
e le vestali avevano corolle
sempre accese nel grembo,
tu vivevi di già poi che veduta
t'ho nel sonno e vagante, sconcertata
urgevi già alle porte dell'amore
senza averne risposta. Ira conclusa
musica folle inetta alle fatiche
della Grecia gaudente e pur ben salda
dentro la luce enorme che ti tiene.
Sempre, Violetta, il tempo ti oscurava
dentro quella mordente nostalgia
di cose pure, nate dal pensiero
purificate al vivo nel dolore . . .
E sempre sola, come una puledra
di sceltissima razza, pascolando
riluttante le biade degli umani
ardi d'amore come un giglio chiuso . . .

DREAM

During the infinite time of Greece
when paradise was given over
to the girls in warm gardens
and the vestals held ever-glowing
crowns in their wombs,
you were already alive for I had
seen you sleep-walking, I was taken aback
you were already pressing against love's doors
without any answer. Settled-down rage
mad music of reveling Greece
incapable of toil and yet steady
in the enormous light that holds you.
Always, Violetta, the time that shadows you
within that biting nostalgia
for pure things, born out of thought
and purified in pain's reality . . .
And always alone, like a thoroughbred
mare out to pasture,
rejecting the fodder men offer
you burn for love like a closed lily . . .

LIRICA ANTICA

Caro, dammi parole di fiducia
per te, mio uomo, l'unico che amassi
in lunghi anni di stupido terrore,
fa che le mani m'escano dal buio
incantesimo amaro che non frutta . . .
Sono gioielli, vedi, le mie mani,
sono un linguaggio per l'amore vivo
ma una fosca catena le ha ben chiuse
ben legate ad un ceppo. Amore mio
ho sognato di te come si sogna
della rosa e del vento,
sei purissimo, vivo, un equilibrio
astrale, ma io sono nella notte
e non posso ospitarti. Io vorrei
che tu gustassi i pascoli che in dono
ho sortiti da Dio, ma la paura
mi trattiene nemica; oso parole,
solamente parole e se tu ascolti
fiducioso il mio canto, veramente
so che ti esalterai delle mie pene.

Antique Lyric

Dear, give me words of trust
for you, my man, the only one I ever loved
in long years of stupid terror,
make my hands escape the dark
bitter spell that bears no fruit . . .
They are jewels, you see, my hands,
they are a language for living love
but a sullied chain locked them tight
and tied them to a stump. My love
I dreamed of you as someone dreams
of the rose and of the wind,
you the purest, alive, an alignment
of the stars, but I am in the night
and cannot shelter you. I wish
that you could taste the meadows that, as a gift,
God sent to me, but fear
holds me back like an enemy; I dare words,
only words, and if you listen
trusting to my song, truly
I know that you will be lifted away by my suffering.

E PIÚ FACILE ANCORA

E piú facile ancora mi sarebbe
scendere a te per le piú buie scale,
quelle del desiderio che mi assalta
come lupo infecondo nella notte.

So che tu coglieresti dei miei frutti
con le mani sapienti del perdono . . .

E so anche che mi ami di un amore
casto, infinito, regno di tristezza . . .

Ma io il pianto per te l'ho levigato
giorno per giorno come luce piena
e lo rimando tacita ai miei occhi
che, se ti guardo, vivono di stelle.

And It Would Be Even Easier

And it would be even easier for me
to come down to you by the darkest stair,
that one out of the desire that assaults me
like a barren wolf in the night.

I know that you would pluck my fruits
with the wise hands of forgiveness ...

And I also know that you love me with a love
chaste, infinite, realm of sadness ...

As for my crying over you, I bleached it away slowly
day by day as full light does
and in silence I sent it back to my eyes,
which, if I look at you, are alive with stars.

[IO ERO UN UCCELLO]

Io ero un uccello
dal bianco ventre gentile,
qualcuno mi ha tagliato la gola
          per riderci sopra,
          non so.
Io ero un albatro grande
e volteggiavo sui mari.
Qualcuno ha fermato il mio viaggio,
senza nessuna carità di suono.
Ma anche distesa per terra
io canto ora per te
le mie canzoni d'amore.

[AS FOR ME, I USED TO BE A BIRD]

As for me, I used to be a bird
with a gentle white womb,
someone cut my throat
        just for laughs,
        I don't know.
As for me, I used to be a great albatross
and whirled over the seas.
Someone put an end to my journey,
without any charity in the tone of it.
But even stretched out on the ground
I sing for you now
my songs of love.

TANGENZIALE DELL'OVEST

Tangenziale dell'ovest,
scendi dai tuoi vertici profondi,
squarta questi ponti di rovina,
allunga il passo e rimuovi
le antiche macerie della Porta,
sicché si tendano gli ampi valloni
e la campagna si schiuda.
Tangenziale dell'ovest,
queste acque amare debbono morire,
non vi veleggia alcuno, né lontano
senti il rimbombo del risanamento,
butta questi ponti di squarcio
dove pittori isolati
muoiono un mutamento;
qui la nuda ringhiera che ti afferra
è una parabola d'oriente
accecata dal masochismo,
qui non pullula alcuna scienza,
ma muore tutto putrefatto conciso
con una lama di crimine azzurro
con un bisturi folle
che fa di questi paraggi
la continuazione dell'ovest,
dove germina Villa Fiorita.

WESTERN RING ROAD

Western ring road,
come down from your deep heights,
cut through these collapsing bridges,
take a longer step and clear away
the derelict buildings by the Porta Ticinese
so that wide valleys might be even wider
and the fields might disclose themselves.
Western ring road,
these bitter waters must die,
no one sails and, from far away, you do not
hear the booming echo of recovery,
launch these bridges ripping apart
where lonely painters
perish in transformation;
here the naked railing that grasps you
is an eastern parabola
blinded by masochism,
here not a single knowledge pulses,
but everything rotten concise dies
with a blade of blue crime
with a crazy scalpel
that makes of this neighborhood
the extension of the west,
where Villa Fiorita sprouts.

[La luna s'apre nei giardini del manicomio]

La luna s'apre nei giardini del manicomio,
qualche malato sospira,
      mano nella tasca nuda.
            La luna chiede tormento
            e chiede sangue ai reclusi:
    ho visto un malato
    morire dissanguato
            sotto la luna accesa.

[THE MOON UNVEILS ITSELF IN THE MADHOUSE GARDENS]

The moon unveils itself in the madhouse gardens,
some patients sigh,
      a hand in the nude pocket.
            The moon demands torments
            and exacts blood of the inmates
I have seen a patient
dying from shed blood
      beneath the shining moon.

[IL MIO PRIMO TRAFUGAMENTO DI MADRE]

Il mio primo trafugamento di madre
avvenne in una notte d'estate
quando un pazzo mi prese
e mi adagiò sopra l'erba
e mi fece concepire un figlio.
O mai la luna gridò cosí tanto
contro le stelle offese,
e mai gridarono tanto i miei visceri,
né il Signore volse mai il capo all'indietro
come in quell'istante preciso
vedendo la mia verginità di madre
offesa dentro a un ludibrio.
Il mio primo trafugamento di donna
avvenne in un angolo oscuro
sotto il calore impetuoso del sesso,
ma nacque una bimba gentile
con un sorriso dolcissimo
e tutto fu perdonato.
Ma io non perdonerò mai
e quel bimbo mi fu tolto dal grembo
e affidato a mani piú "sante",
ma fui io ad essere oltraggiata,
io che salii sopra i cieli
per avere concepito una genesi.

[MY FIRST MOTHER-THEFT]

My first mother-theft
took place on a summer night
when a madman took me
and laid me on the grass
and forced me to conceive a son.
Oh never did the moon cry so much
against the violated stars,
and never did my womb cry so much,
and the Lord never turned away his head
as he did in that precise instant
seeing my mother-virginity
violated, treated as his laughing stock.
My first woman-theft
took place in a dark corner
under the vehement heat of sex,
but a gentle baby girl was born
with the sweetest smile
and everything was forgiven.
Nevertheless I myself will never forgive
and that son was taken away from my womb
and entrusted into more "saintly" hands,
nevertheless I was the one who was offended,
I was the one who climbed above the heavens
for having conceived a genesis.

IL CANTO DELLO SPÓSO

Forse tu hai dentro il tuo corpo
    un seme di grande ragione,
ma le tue labbra gaudenti
    che sanno di tanta ironia
    hanno morso piú baci
      di quanto ne voglia il Signore,
    come si morde una mela
      al colmo della pienezza.
E le tue mani roventi
    nude, di maschio deciso
    hanno dato piú abbracci
    di quanto ne valga una messe,
    eppure il mio cuore ti canta,
      o sposo novello
      eppure in me è la sorpresa
      di averti accanto a morire
      dopo che un fiume di vita
      ti ha spinto all'argine pieno.

The Song of the Groom

Perhaps you have inside your body
    a seed of great reason,
but your ardent lips
    that taste of so much irony
    have bitten more kisses
        than the Lord might want,
    just as someone bites an apple
        at the peak of its fullness.
And your burning hands
    naked, of resolute masculinity
    handed out more embraces
    than a harvest is worth,
    even so my heart sings of you,
        oh my fresh groom
        even so in me there's the surprise
        that you will lie next to me dying
        after a river of life
        has pushed you up against the levees.

Elegia

O la natura degli angeli azzurri,
i cerchi delle loro ali felici,
ne vidi mai nei miei sogni?
O sí, quando ti amai,
quando ho desiderato di averti,
o i pinnacoli dolci del paradiso,
le selve del turbamento,
quando io vi entrai anima aperta,
lacerata di amore,
o i sintomi degli angeli di Dio,
i dolorosi tornaconti del cuore.
Anima aperta, ripara le ali:
io viaggio dentro l'immenso
e l'immenso turba le mie ciglia.
Ho visto un angelo dolce
ghermire il tuo dolce riso
e portarmelo nella bocca.

ELEGY

Oh, the nature of the blue angels,
the ringing circles of their happy wings,
have I ever seen any of them in my dreams?
Oh yes, when I used to love you,
when I wanted so much to possess you,
or the sweet pinnacles of paradise,
the troubled woods,
when I stepped in as an open soul,
lacerated by love,
or the symptoms of God's angels,
the heart's painful returns.
Open soul, repair your wings:
I travel inside the immensity
and the immensity troubles my eyelashes.
I saw a sweet angel
grab your sweet smile
and carry it to my mouth.

SAFFO

O diletta, da cui compitai il mio lungo commento,
o donna straordinaria vela che adduci ad un porto
o storica magia o dolce amara
essenza delle muse coronate
di viole e fiori, viola pur tu stessa,
perché mai l'abbacinante sgomento
di un amore ingiustamente negato?

SAPPHO

O beloved, from whom I slowly learn to finish all my
      homework,
oh extraordinary woman sail who shows the way to a
      port of arrival
oh historical magic oh sweet bitter
essence of muses crowned
with violets and flowers, you yourself a violet,
why on earth the most dismaying dazzling
of an unfairly denied love?

EMILY DICKINSON

Emily Dickinson patentata quacquera,
inutile mettere muri tra te e le parole
e le svenevolezze della sorella
pronte ai tuoi inverosimili deliqui.
La forza si immette nella forza
la spada dentro la terra.

EMILY DICKINSON

Emily Dickinson certified Quaker,
it's pointless to build walls between you and words
and the whooziness of the sister
ready for your unlikely swooning.
Strength inserts itself in strength
the spade into the earth.

PLATH

Povera Plath troppo alta per le miserie della terra,
meglio certamente la morte
e un forno crematorio
alle continue bruciature del vento,
meglio Silvia l'avveniristica impresa
di una donna che voleva essere donna
che è stata scalpitata da un uomo femmina.

PLATH

Wretched Plath too high for the miseries of the earth,
certainly death is better
and a crematorium's furnace
is better than the unending burning of the wind,
better Sylvia the adventurous enterprise
of a woman who wanted to be a woman
who got all riled up over a female man.

ALDA MERINI

Amai teneramente dei dolcissimi amanti
senza che essi sapessero mai nulla.
E su questi intessei tele di ragno
e fui preda della mia stessa materia.
In me l'anima c'era della meretrice
della santa della sanguinaria e dell'ipocrita.
Molti diedero al mio modo di vivere un nome
e fui soltanto una isterica.

ALDA MERINI

I tenderly loved some very sweet lovers
without them knowing anything about it.
And I wove spiderwebs from this
and I always fell prey to my own creation.
In me there was the soul of the prostitute
of the saint of the one who lusts for blood and of the
        hypocrite.
Many people gave a label to my way of life
and all that while I was only an hysteric.

IL PASTRANO

Un certo pastrano abitò lungo tempo in casa
era un pastrano di lana buona
un pettinato leggero
un pastrano di molte fatture
vissuto e rivoltato mille volte
era il disegno del nostro babbo
la sua sagoma ora assorta ed ora felice.
Appeso a un cappio o al portabiti
assumeva un'aria sconfitta:
traverso quell'antico pastrano
ho conosciuto i segreti di mio padre
vivendolo cosí, nell'ombra.

THE OVERCOAT

A certain overcoat lived at our house for a long time
it was made of good wool
a finely-combed wool
a many-times-made-over overcoat
well-worn, a thousand times turned inside out
it wore the outline of our father
his very figure, whether worried or happy.
Hanging on a hook or on the coat rack
it took on a defeated air:
through that ancient overcoat
I came to know my father's secrets
to live that life, in the shadow.

IL GREMBIULE

Mia madre invece aveva un vecchio grembiule
per la festa e il lavoro,
a lui si consolava vivendo.
In quel grembiule noi trovammo ristoro
fu dato agli straccivendoli
dopo la morte, ma un barbone
riconoscendone la maternità
ne fece un molle cuscino
per le sue esequie vive.

THE APRON

My mother, though, had an old apron
for holidays and work,
and she consoled herself with it by living.
We found solace in that apron
that was given away to the ragmen
after her death, but a tramp,
recognizing its maternity,
made a soggy pillow from it
for his living funeral rites.

L'OSPITE

Ti sei presentato una sera ubriaco
sollevando l'audace gesto
di chi vuole fare cadere una donna
nel proprio tranello oscuro
e io non ti ho creduto
profittatore infingardo.
Sulla mia buona fede
avresti lasciato cadere il tuo inguine sporco;
per tanta tua malizia
hai commesso un reato morto.

THE GUEST

You showed up one night drunk
jacking up the audacious gesture
of someone who wants to make a woman fall
into his own dark snare
and I didn't trust you
you untrustworthy opportunist.
Over my good faith
you would have let your dirty groin fall
despite all your guile
you committed a still-born crime.

[Cesare amò Cleopatra]

Cesare amò Cleopatra,
io amo Pierri divino
che non conduce nessuna guerra,
che è solo condottiero di nostalgia,
ma il mio letto povero
giace nel solstizio d'estate
ed è un audace triclinio
quando lui a sera in vena d'amore
mi dice parole di patriottismo segreto.

[Caesar loved Cleopatra]

Caesar loved Cleopatra,
I love divine Pierri
who commands no war,
who is only a commander of nostalgia,
but my poor bed
lies in the summer solstice
and it is an audacious divan
when at evening in the mood for love
he tells me words of our secret patriotism.

OTELLO

Otello, Otello dalla voce rossa,
quaggiú non è piú tempo di riscossa;
dalle verdi vallate della morte
alla tua sposa tu hai cambiato sorte.
Cerco l'ombra degli inferi profonda
e la palude mi diventa bionda;
altra donna ti è accanto,
altra natura
e tu mi hai rinchiuso nelle scaltre mura.

OTHELLO

Othello, red-voiced Othello,
there's no more time to turn the tide below:
between death's valleys, so green,
and your wife, you changed the scheme.
I look for the deep shadow of that demimonde,
and find the swamp, from here, turns blonde;
another woman is next to you,
another nature
and within its cunning walls, you locked me as a
    prisoner.

LA SOTTOVESTE

Lungamente interrogata e stretta
da vincoli tremendi
se avessi avuto un futuro di pace
o un futuro di guerra.
Mi lasciai scivolare la sottoveste
da entrambe le spalle.
Per la verità le trovarono lisce
come quelle di una bambina.
Ma trovarono torpido il mio cervello
che aveva amato.
Videro i fiori della mia carne
e dissero che ero incorrotta.
Ma quel cencio strappatomi via
da tante e tante ferite
se lo contesero in molti.
La mia nudità fu la mia vergogna,
per tutta la vita,
e mi scomparve Orfeo per sempre.

THE SLIP

For a long time interrogated and bound
by tremendous chains
as to whether I would have a peaceful future
or a warring one.
I let my slip slip down
from both my shoulders.
In truth they found them
as smooth as a baby girl's.
But they found my brain was
sluggish from so much loving.
They saw the flowers of my flesh
and said I was uncorrupted.
But that stripped-away rag
from many, many a wound
plenty of them fought over it.
My nudity became my shame,
throughout my whole life
and Orpheus vanished from me forever.

[TORNAI ALLORA A QUELLA NEVE CHIARA]

Tornai allora a quella neve chiara
che arrossava i miei guanti nella notte,
quando da sola e per ben corta via
venivo a rintracciare la speranza.

Non volevo i tuoi carmi, non volevo
chiedere ad altri dov'io fossi nata
ma perché la disgrazia cosí bieca
si trastullasse con le mie povere forze.
Entrambi divorati dal pudore
ci trattenemmo fermi per tre anni
pieni di sgominevoli peccati
e non fummo nemmeno grandi santi
né grandi peccatori longobardi:
fu una guerra politica e sociale,
una guerra di orrore dei confini,
una guerra piegata dalla fame.

[THEN I WENT BACK TO THAT BRIGHT SNOW]

Then I went back to that bright snow
that turned my gloves red in the night,
when alone and through a shortcut,
I used to come to retrace hope.

I didn't want your songs, I didn't want
to ask anyone else where I was born
but instead why such a black disgrace
toyed with my poor strengths.
Both of us devoured by pain
we steadied ourselves firmly for three years
filled with crushing sins
and we were neither great saints
nor great Longobardian sinners;
it was a political and social war,
a war of horror over borderlines,
a war hedged about by hunger.

[CHE INSOSTENIBILE CHIAROSCURO]

Che insostenibile chiaroscuro,
mutevole concetto di ogni giorno,
parola d'ordine che dice: non vengo
e ti lascio morire poco a poco.

Perché questa lentezza del caos?
Perché il verbo non mi avvicina?
Perché non mangio i frammenti di ieri
come se fosse un futuro d'amore?

[WHAT UNBEARABLE CHIAROSCURO]

What unbearable chiaroscuro,
shifting concept of every day,
password that says: I'm not coming
and I'm letting you die little by little.

Why this slowing of chaos?
Why doesn't the word come close to me?
Why don't I eat the fragments of yesterday
as if it were a future filled with love?

AFORISMI

Non sempre
si riesce
ad essere
eterni.

Il poeta
che vede tutto
viene accusato
di libertà
di pensiero.

Gusto il peccato come fosse
il principio del benessere.

Il paradiso non mi piace
perché verosimilmente non ha ossessioni.

Io amo perché
il mio corpo
è sempre
in evoluzione.

Non mi lascio mai
escludere
dal mio io.

Le voglie erotiche
sono sempre riferite a un palinsesto.

Aphorisms

Not always
does one manage
to be
eternal.

The poet
who sees everything
is accused
of freedom
of thought.

I enjoy sin as if it were
the beginning of well-being.

Paradise does not please me
because so far as I can see it has no obsessions.

I am in love because
my body
is always
in evolution.

I never let myself
be excluded
from myself.

Erotic desires
always point to a palimpsest.

La calunnia
è un vocabolo sdentato
che quando arriva
a destinazione
mette mandibole di ferro.

Ci sono notti
che non
accadono mai.

Non si sa mai
quanto sia lunga
la lingua
degli innamorati.

Calumny
is a toothless word
that, once it arrives
at its destination,
puts on iron jaws.

There are nights
that never
happen.

One never knows
how lingering
they are, the tongues
of lovers.

from *Superba è la notte*

[SULLA NOCE DI UN'ALBICOCCA]

Sulla noce di un'albicocca
sul primo pensiero che mi salta in mente
fondo l'alluce della ragione
per toccare i tuoi piedi eterni.

[ON THE PIT OF AN APRICOT]

On the pit of an apricot
on the first thought that pops into my mind
I establish reason's big toe
so I can touch your eternal feet.

[La cosa più superba è la notte]

La cosa più superba è la notte
quando cadono gli ultimi spaventi
e l'anima si getta all'avventura.
Lui tace nel tuo grembo
come riassorbito dal sangue
che finalmente si colora di Dio
e tu preghi che taccia per sempre
per non sentirlo come un rigoglio fisso
fin dentro le pareti.

[THE MOST SUPERB THING IS THE NIGHT]

The most superb thing is the night
when the last threats tumble
and the soul throws itself into adventure.
As for him, he is silent in your womb
as if reabsorbed by blood
that finally takes on the color of God
and you pray that he will always be silent
so you won't hear him as a steady gurgling
even inside the walls.

[LA NOTTE SE NON È RAPIDA]

a E. C.

La notte se non è rapida
non fa in tempo a coprire il sogno.
Lanterne sono i miei occhi e tu
il fiato che le appanna.
Dormi sul cuore di tutti
o piccolo asfodelo
e non appena le unghie
avranno scalfito il gelo dell'inverno
tornerai tu ranuncolo pieno
a rendermi felice.
Avide le tue coppe di avorio
avidi i testicoli del desiderio
e le dita piene di prugne
ingemmano i vasti odori.

[Night, if it is not swift]

for E. C.

Night, if it is not swift
has no time to cover the dream.
My eyes are lanterns and you
the breath that clouds them.
You sleep on everyone's heart
oh little asphodel
and as soon as the fingernails
have scraped the winter cold
you will return you blossoming arunculus
to make me happy.
Eager your ivory cups
eager your testicles of desire
and the fingers filled with plums
blossom into vast perfumes.

[C'ERA UNA FONTANA CHE DAVA ALBE]

C'era una fontana che dava albe
ed ero io.
Al mattino appena svegliata
avevo vento di fuoco
e cercavo di capire da che parte
volasse la poesia.
Adesso ahimè tutti vogliono
strapparmi la veste,
ahimè come ero felice
quando inseguivo i delitti
di questa porta dalle mille paure.
Adesso tutto è deserto e solo,
gemono ventiquattro cancelli
su cardini ormai spenti.

[THERE WAS A FOUNTAIN THAT OFFERED DAWNS]

There was a fountain that offered dawns
and that was I.
In the morning, just awakened,
I used to hold a fiery wind
and I tried to determine the direction
where poetry would fly.
Now alas everyone wants
to tear my clothes off,
alas how happy I was
when I used to chase down the crimes
of this door of a thousand fears.
And now everything is deserted and lonely,
twenty-four gates creak
on the by-now-dead posts.

[NAVIGLIO CHE SOCCORRI LA MIA CARNE]

Naviglio che soccorri la mia carne
essa è una nave che ha saggiato
molti porti e lasciato molti figli
nell'abbraccio di ossuti marinai.
Eppure come me del vello d'oro
nessuno sa mai nulla. Incorniciata
la fronte di frescure inusitate
batto i denti nel freddo meridiano
dove adagio si stendono le suore.

[NAVIGLIO THAT SUCCORS MY FLESH]

Naviglio that succors my flesh
it is a ship that tasted
many ports and abandoned many children
to the embrace of skinny sailors.
However no one ever knows anything
like I do about the golden fleece.
My forehead is framed by awkward breezes
my teeth chatter in the mid-day cold
where, slowly, the nuns lie down for their nap.

[CI SONO I PARADISI ARTIFICIALI]

Ci sono i paradisi artificiali
e vengono lenti dalla lontananza
del Nord. Ho visto un coccodrillo
baciare le frontiere e pascolare
con Orfeo sconvolto tra le braccia.

[THERE ARE ARTIFICIAL PARADISES]

There are artificial paradises
and they come slowly from the distance
of the North. I have seen a crocodile
kissing the frontiers and grazing in the pasture
with a shocked Orpheus between his arms.

[RESTI UN ARDENTE ULIVO]

a Barbara

Resti un ardente ulivo
che mi dà la penombra
e mi scaldo al ricordo di come fui
quando amavo i tuoi pallidi sentieri.
Eccomi, stuolo bugiardo di occhi
lungo il pavone della tua certezza.
Sei fine sentimento di menzogna
quando mi ascolti ridere.

[Stay steady burning olive tree]

for Barbara

Stay steady burning olive tree
that gives me a little shadow
as I warm up remembering how I was
when I loved your fading pathways.
Here I am, a lying parade of eyes
across the peacock of your certainty.
You are a refined feeling of falsity
when you listen to me as I laugh.

IN MORTE DI MIA SORELLA

O anima che scavi la terra
adesso giustamente perduta
resta in noi il tuo modesto cammino,
anima di sempre: ascolta
ora il nostro babelico linguaggio
colmato di silenzio,
tu che sei ormai santa parola
e forse parola imperfetta
ma che certo cammini sull'acqua
col piede di un amante.

On the Death of My Sister

O soul who digs in the earth
now truly lost
keep your modest path in us,
soul of always: listen
now to our babbling language
brimming with silence,
you who are by now perfected word
and perhaps imperfect word
but who surely walks on water
with the feet of a lover.

[O CANTO DELLA NEVE CHIUSO DENTRO LA FOSSA]

ad Anna Merini Bertassello

O canto della neve chiuso dentro la fossa
leggiadro il paradiso che correva sull'acqua
con l'inguine perfetto che declama le sfere
e nuca di cordoglio era la tua cavezza
di giovane che salta le barriere del sonno
e invano nella cruda finestra della vita
gettasti il coperchio di tante tue imposture
e oggi avanzi in cielo come donna superba,
mentre fosti una siepe, una roccia, una vita,
simile al coraggio che animò le tue onde.
Ora vivi rapita nel suono delle dita,
ampie misure d'aria che solcano i presepi
sorella di domanda che si infrange sull'acqua
e simile a parola tu abiti il destino,
fai soffrire la folla che chiede il tuo mistero.

[OH SONG OF THE SNOW STUCK INSIDE THE DITCH]

to Anna Merini Bertassello

Oh song of the snow stuck inside the ditch
light-hearted paradise that ran above water
with perfect loins declaiming the spheres
and sorrow's nape was your chafing halter
when as a young woman you leaped the barriers of sleep
and in vain threw into the raw window of life
the lid of your many impostures
and today you ascend to the stars like a movie star,
while in truth you were a hedge, a rock, a life,
something like the courage that set your waves in
        motion.
Now you live captivated within the play of fingers
wide measures of air that cut through the crèches
sister of a question that breaks apart on the water
and like a word you inhabit destiny,
you make the crowd that wants your mystery suffer.

GUERRA

O uomo sconciato come una fossa
in te si lavano le mani i servi,
i servi del delitto
che ti cambiano veste parola e udito
che ti fanno simile a un fantasma dorato.
Viscidi uccelli visitano le tue dimore
sparvieri senza volto
ti legano i polsi alle vendette
degli altri
che vogliono dissacrare il Signore.
O guerra, portento di ogni spavento
malvagità inarcata, figlia stretta
generata dal suolo di nessuno
non hai udito né ombra:
sei un mostro senza anima che mangia
la soglia
e il futuro dell'uomo.

WAR

O man ruined like a ditch
servants wash their hands in you,
the servants of murder
who change your clothes your words your hearing
who turn you into a golden ghost.
Slimy birds visit your dwellings
faceless sparrows
tie your wrists to the vendettas
of those
who want to desecrate God.
O war, prophet of all fear
overarching evil, true daughter
born of no one's ground
you have neither hearing nor shadow:
you are a soulless monster eating
the threshold
and future of man.

IL CORVO

Il mattino era devastante come l'annunciazione
della follia e gravava sopra i visceri
delle foglie come se una mano fredda e tagliente
stroncasse la doppia vita
degli amanti. Erano tempi in cui la mia memoria
confusa vagava di sospiro in sospiro
di lutto in lutto
e la vita faceva fatica ad emergere dal sonno come
un nero pulviscolo di morte e tutto era cosí
portato avanti da un divino sapere
che sfuggiva e languiva nelle mie stesse mani.
Anni pieni di colpa e diluvio, anni che venivano
a sapere che io avevo cominciato
il mio rito e le mie paure e questo
orribile portatore di male
che è il destino saliva sulla mia schiena
come un cavallo sudaticcio e inverecondo
che volesse falsare le carte e portare
alla rovina il Signore di tutte le cose . . .
Questi cadaveri cupi e sommessi
che riempiono l'aria con le loro forcine
e le loro grida, traendo donne insane per i capelli
e vendemmiatori astuti,
questa incolore magia che è l'universo
piú cupo ahimè di ogni battaglia, io che divento il
        dicitore
della mia stessa sconfitta e il retroscena di una battaglia
onirica. Il tempo di questa illusione perduta in cui
i peccati di lui e di lei sono venuti a cadere sopra
il mio peccato coprendolo di insulti

The Raven

The morning was as devastating as the annunciation
of madness and weighed down on the veins
of the leaves as if a cold sharp hand
would cleave the lovers' double
life. There were times when my confused
memory was wandering from sigh to sigh
from mourning to mourning
and life struggled to emerge from sleep like
a black mote of death and everything was
carried forward by a divine knowledge
that was slipping away and vanishing from my own
    hands.
Years filled with guilt and floods, years that came
to know that I had begun
my rite and my fears and this
horrible bearer of evil
that is destiny was climbing on my back
like a sweaty shameful little horse
that might want to cheat and carry
off to ruin the Lord of everything . . .
These somber and modest corpses
that fill the air with their bobbypins
and their cries, dragging insane women by the hair
and shrewd toilers in the vineyard,
this colorless magic that is the universe
more somber alas than every battle, I who turn into the
    reciter
of my own defeat and the background of a battle
of dreams. The length of this lost illusion in which
the sins of him and the sins of her came to fall above
my own sin showering it with insults

e di miserie, questa istantanea rottura con l'universo
dove io da pacifica divento fredda come l'alba
e sorniona come la morte in un duplice omicidio
che sta tra pelle e pelle
tra presenza e presenza. Il fare vecchio
di questo annuncio di vita che diventa
escremento di ogni grandezza. Il mio naturale
stupore è tutto ciò che è carne consolidata
carne eguale in tutto alle zolle
di questo divino insulto.
UN CORVO.
È lui l'impietoso uccello che gonfiava le ali del suo
abbandono, che pareva frenetico incontro
alla morte che usciva dalle sue stesse urla
come un frammento di grido
che doveva essere spettacolare e orrendo
intorno ai capelli di una ninfa cosí
colorata cosí fresca cosí invidiosa della felicità
altrui e tutte queste dolci aperture che
franavano nel freddo delle mie mani
scardinate dalla vita medesima, mani inconsulte
che addomesticavano i sogni come tanti agnelli
nel corpo grasso di Ulisse. Queste angeliche grida
che traversavano il passo come lame
incandescenti che rendevano folle
il mio abbandono e soprattutto il piacere
di essere totalmente nudi dentro questo rovistio
di carte che faceva il corpo affettuoso
e pusillanime portando oltre il mio
infanticidio segreto quello di una
bambina che nel sonno diventa
un forte poeta.

and miseries, this sudden break with the universe
where I who was calm turn as cold as the dawn
and stubbornly sleepily resistant as death in a double
    homicide
that lies between skin and skin
between presence and presence. The old formation
of this sign of life that becomes
the excrement of every greatness. My natural
wonder is all that is solid flesh
flesh that is equal in everything to the clods
of this divine insult.
A RAVEN.
It's he the merciless bird that pumped up the wings of his
abandonment, who seemed to death like
a frenetic encounter that was released from its own cries
as a fragment of a scream
meant to be spectacular and horrifying
around the hair of a nymph so
colorful so fresh so envious of someone else's happiness
and all these sweet openings that
crumbled in the cold of my hands
crow-barred from life itself, unusual hands
that tamed dreams as many lambs
were tamed in the fat body of Ulysses. These angelic
    screams
that cut through the path like hot metal blades
driving mad
my abandonment and above all the pleasure
of being totally nude within this rifled-through pile
of papers that made the body affectionate
and cowardly furthering my
secret infanticide, that of
a small girl who in her sleep becomes
a strong poet.

Il grido della morte

ad A.M.B.

Qui dove abito non si sente nulla di nulla, nemmeno il
   grido
della morte, il paradosso oscuro che scivola via dalla vita
quell'ingorgo che può fare presagire il passato, quel
   vuoto
di memoria assoluto che porta al compimento di ogni
   parola.
Niente affoga il passato, niente lo risolleva dal suo
baratro, nessuna incertezza è dentro il sonno e nessuna
   ora
fu piú velata e piú martoriata di questa che arde
nel silenzio di un'ermetica chiusura di porte che non si
   aprono
e non si concedono al canto. Il male è una fossa
   tremenda,
l'ateo pruriginoso del nostro solco di vita. Ecco anche
il male rimane incerto e sospeso in questo
non essere presenti al male medesimo della vita.
Nessuno che pianga o si discolpi o che diventi
   personaggio
e figura nel tempio della morte, nessuna meretrice che
balzi spontanea al canto della strada, a soffrire e a offrire
il bene del suo ventre disfatto per andare oltre i confini
della parola. Nessuna canzone muliebre o sofferta che
   abbia
in sé radici malsane o comunque radici di vita, e nessun
velo che possa alzarsi come figura e che diventi aiuola e

The Cry of Death

for A.M.B.

Here where I live you can't hear anything at all, not even
    the cry
of death, obscure paradox that slips away from life
that chokes, that could make someone forecast the past,
    that absolute
void of memory that leads to the fulfilment of every
    word.
Nothing sinks the past, nothing lifts it from its
pit, no uncertainty lies within sleep and no time
was ever more veiled and more martyred than this one
    that burns
in the silence of doors secretly closing that do not open
and do not give themselves up to poetry. Evil is a terrible
    ditch,
the itchy atheist of our life's furrow. Look, even
evil remains uncertain and suspended in this
absence from life's very same evil.
No one would cry or exonerate himself or become a
    character
and figure in the temple of death, no prostitute
would jump spontaneously to the side of the street, to
    suffer and to offer
the smashed fruit of her womb as a way to get beyond
    the confines
of the word. No woman's song or song of suffering
    would have
in itself rotten roots or in any case roots of life, and no
veil that could lift itself like a figure and turn into a
    flowerbed and

117

che diventi fatica. Anche la fatica di amare, perenne
dolcezza della vita, è stata scaricata da una parsimonia
     infelice.
Gli uomini sono come velieri, velieri immoti che non
solcano acque, che non risanano il linguaggio,
gli uomini sono occasioni di vendemmia, ma niente altro.
Essi potrebbero apparire e sparire dalla fama
del grande albero della vita come i sogni, e potrebbero
portare con sé il nostro linguaggio infantile
fatto di occasioni tremende. La nostra fantasia si
incammina nel cielo, essa è colpevole come la parola
e il silenzio medesimo di questi orribili portatori
di frane che gravitano sopra un letto, accesi di colpa
e inerenti proprio al male piú prodigiosamente
satanici di colui che afferra il coltello e apre la chiave
scurrile di una porta che si chiama vita, per lasciarne
uscire l'anima affogata nelle lacrime e nel sapere.
Sono proprio questi uomini scorrevoli come la
     dannazione
eterna, che cacciano il peccato dalle loro mitiche
lenzuola di presagio per dar corso alla fama di colei
che fruttuosamente godeva del peccato peggiore che è
l'azione. Dentro il peccato esseri ingobbiti nelle loro
     tenebre
sussultano al primo apparire della notte, come se la colpa
fosse consapevole in loro e l'anima traviata
potesse cadere addosso alla loro ridondanza.
Fiaccole infelici e vane che vanno oltre questa
posa di pietra che è la vita e che giace
nel tentacolo amaro della solitudine, come se volesse
prendere il principio di ogni radice, e colei che
ingemmava il suo sapere e la sua fama di donna, ora

turn into fatigue. Even the fatigue of loving, the perennial
sweetness of life, has been discarded by an unhappy
     stinginess.
Men are like three-masters, ships unmoved that don't
plow the water, that don't heal the language,
men are moments of harvesting the vineyard, but
     nothing more.
They could appear and disappear from the fame
of the great tree of life like dreams, and they could
carry within themselves our babbling
made up of terrible moments. Our fantasy
sets out toward the sky, it is as guilty as the word
or the very same silence of those horrible porters
of avalanches who hover above a bed, lit with guilt
and precisely involved in the most prodigiously satanic
kind of evil like the one who grabs the knife and opens
     the scurrilous
key of a door called life, in order to release
the soul that sunk into tears and into knowing.
It is these very slippery men like eternal
damnation, who hunt sin from their mythic
prophetic bed-sheets to give way to the fame of she who
fruitfully enjoyed the worst sin—that is,
the actual deed. Within sin creatures bowed over by their
     own darkness
startle at the first appearance of night, as if guilt
were conscious within them and the corrupted soul
might trip over their own redundancy.
Unhappy and vain torches that reach beyond this
stony pose that is life lying
in the bitter tentacle of solitude, as if it wanted
to grasp the beginning of every root, and she who
embellishes her knowing and her reputation as a woman,
     now

è passata a tenebre sicure, lei che faceva l'inventario
della mia morte ora per ora, trascinandola per
i capelli come fosse stata l'esempio stesso
di un cuore spettacolare fatto di marciume e di solitudine
che porta male, che porta solamente silenzio.
Il male quindi se ne è andato in un vecchio sapere delle
        cose
in un ancheggiare fosco che porta lontano i nostri
        pensieri
e li fa grigi come la notte, e come il parto infelice di una
musa cieca e sorda che non ha un'aiuola fiorita
che non vuole presagire nulla se non la notte e la fatica
mortuaria del senso, pare che diventi il proprio
crimine orrendo. Qui sul ballatoio infelice, la donna
di nessun esempio e di nessuna paura giace velata per
sempre in un'ovazione generale che ha visto cadere
il dubbio della fortuna e la fortuna del dubbio.

has been passed into enduring darkness, she who kept
    the inventory
of my death hour by hour, dragging it by
the hair as if it were the very epitome
of a spectacular heart made of rot and solitude
bringing bad luck, bringing only silence.
Evil therefore has gone into an old knowledge of things
in an obscure swaying of hips that carries away our
    thoughts
and makes them as gray as night, and like the unhappy
    birth of
a blind and deaf muse who has no flowering bush
who does not prophesy anything but the night and a
    deadly
exhaustion of meaning, it seems to become someone's
    own
horrible crime. Here on the unhappy veranda, the
    woman
who is no model and who has no fear lies veiled for-
ever in a popular ovation that already has seen collapse
the doubt of luck and the luck of doubt.

[NELLA TERRA DI SCOZIA]

a Brunella Antomarini

Nella terra di Scozia
un vecchio proverbio inglese
dice che sotto la terra
è vanno cercare moneta
eppure per una moneta
molti di fanno la guerra.
La faccia di un re feroce
che è solo il Dio destino.
Io giro da molti anni
con questa orrenda bestia
che ho imparato ad amare
fino dai primi passi.
E lo trovo un agnello
chissà perché la gente
fa cosi disperare.

[IN THE LAND OF SCOTLAND]

for Brunella Antomarini

In the land of Scotland
there's an old English proverb
that says that beneath the dirt
it's vain to look for coins,
since because of a single coin
so many will go to war.
The face of a fierce king
who is only the God of destiny.
I have lived for many years
with this horrible beast
I have learned to love
since I took my first steps.
And I find it's a lamb
though who knows why
it drives people to desperation.

NOTES

The poems are printed here in the order of their appearance in *Fiore di poesia 1951–1997*, published by Einaudi in 1998, and *Superba è la notte*, which Einaudi published in 2000. Merini at times places dates beneath the poems, and those are listed here in the notes. Her practice invites us to think of those poems sharing dates as pairs, and those with simply a year as the date as indications of a feeling or thought extending over a longer period of time.

The Presence of Orpheus

Giorgio Manganelli (b. Milano in 1922, d. Rome in 1990) was a novelist and critic. Between 1947 and 1949 he was at the center of a literary circle that included the sixteen-year-old Alda Merini. Manganelli, married and the father of a child, was her lover and mentor during this period, after which he fled Merini and his family for Rome, eventually becoming a prominent figure in the national literary culture. This poem is dated 25 February 1949.

Will I Be Alone?

Dated October 1952.

Mary of Egypt

Tintoretto's oil of 1583–1588 is at the Scuola di San Rocco in Venice.

The poem is dated 26 November 1950. Mary of Egypt—a fourth-century courtesan who converted to Christianity, eventually living a life of solitude in the desert, and associated with several late-life miracles (walking on water, a lion appearing to assist with her burial)—is a figure who combines many of the themes of prostitution and saintliness we find in Merini's work—for example, in the poet's self-portrait.

Peace

Dated 21 April 1954; the notion of "offering" here is not specified, but indicates the bread of the communion rite.

Roman Wedding

Dated 29 December 1948.

The Pietà

Dated 24 November 1951; the title, the Italian word for "compassion," is used for any art work depicting the Virgin Mary with the dead body of Christ, but is particularly associated with two works by Michelangelo devoted to this theme: the 1499 sculpture at St. Peter's and, more relevant to Merini's poem, the unfinished and abstract Rondanini Pietà, which Michelangelo worked on until his death in 1564. The Rondanini Pietà is housed in Milano at the Castello Sforzesco.

The Cumaean Sibyl

Dated 24 November 1951; the Sibyl was the priestess of Apollo at Cumae, near Naples, guide and benefactor of Aeneas in his journey to the underworld. Apollo granted the Sibyl a wish that she might have as many years of life as the grains of sand in a handful, but because she refused to have sex, he simultaneously punished her by denying her eternal youth; she was doomed to wither away until she became only a voice and her uncountable, but finite, years were finished.

When the Anguish

Dated 1954.

Peter's Mission

The poem refers, as my introduction explains, to the theme of Peter's denial of Christ: Matthew 26:34–35, 74–75; Luke 22:34, 60–62; John 13:38, Mark 14:30, 71; John 13:25–27.

The Einaudi editions of Merini's work spell the name of the dedicatee of the poem "Genesi"—the young Sicilian doctor who treated Merini's premature baby daughter, Emanuela (Manuela)—"Pietro de Paschale," yet his published works appear under the name "Pietro di Pasquale."

Dream

Vestal virgins were the only priestesses of ancient Rome, charged with maintaining the fires sacred to Vesta, the goddess of the hearth. The myth of their faithfulness finds its exception in the story of Tarpeia, the vestal virgin who betrayed her countrymen to the Sabines in the hope of being rewarded with gold. Instead she was crushed by the Sabine shields and thrown from the cliff on the south side of the Capitoline—a cliff thereafter known as the "Tarpeian Rock," and scene of ancient executions.

Violetta: Violetta Bisesti, astrologer and literary figure in Milan, a friend of Merini's during the 1950s and early 1960s. In her 2005 memoir, *Sono nata il ventuno a primavera: Diario e nuove poesie*, Merini mentions Besesti also had given her money to support her writing and had helped her publish *Tu sei Pietro*.

[As for me, I used to be a bird]

The albatross here would remind European readers of Baudelaire's poem by that title, though Merini has always claimed that Valéry was her most important influence among French poets.

Western Ring Road

Tangenziale dell'ovest is part of the belt of highways surrounding Milan; Porta (Porta Ticinese): a medieval gate, originally built as part of the circle of walls put up in 1171 after Barbarossa's invasion of Milan, rebuilt by the Visconti family in 1329, and restored in the nineteenth century. The gate is in the vicinity of Merini's apartment in the Naviglio district (see below). Villa Fiorita is a Milanese insane asylum; Merini was sent there, as well as to the hospitals Vergani and Paolo Pini, during periods of madness.

[My first mother-theft]

The expression "Il mio primo trafugamento di madre" is a kind of neologism on the level of the phrase; literally it would be "my first smuggling of mother," where "mother" is a quality or entity, though Merini does not use the word for motherhood, "maternità," a term that would be associated indelibly with women's poetry for obvious reasons, but also as the title of a 1904 volume by Ada Negri.

"The son taken away from my womb": a recent book claims that Merini indeed bore a male child who died prematurely. Franca Pellegrini, *La Tempesta Originale: La Vita di Alda Merini in Poesia*. Firenze: Franco Cesati Editore, 2006, p. 31.

The Song of the Groom

The influence of Ada Negri is apparent in the common imagery and tone of this poem, contemporary to Merini's patronage by Negri's cousin, Silvana Rovelli.

Elegy

"The troubled woods" allude to the opening of Dante's *Inferno*.

Emily Dickinson

Dickinson was not a Quaker, but Merini makes her one here.

Plath

The "crematorium's furnace" refers to the imagery of Plath's poem "Daddy."

[Caesar loved Cleopatra]

Pierri: the poet, writer, and doctor Michele Pierri (b. Naples 1899, d. Taranto 1988). After the death of Merini's first husband, Ettore Carniti, in 1981, the two poets had begun an intense correspondence. In 1983 Pierri and Merini were married in a religious ceremony. Merini moved to Pierri's home in Taranto for three years, but returned to the north in 1986 after a period in the Taranto insane asylum.

Othello

The prevalence of rhyme in Italian makes patterned rhyme comparatively easy and occasional rhyming a feature of most poems in the language. Among Merini's poems offered here, this is perhaps the most strongly rhymed and I have taken some license with its translation in order to emphasize the couplet structure and the force of the single unrhymed line.

[Then I went back to that bright snow]

"Great Longobardian sinners": Milano is part of Lombardy, named for the *Langobardi*, Germanic invaders who invaded northern Italy in 560 and conquered the Roman city of Milan in 569. There is perhaps a folklore of Longobardian lovers that dates to the troubadours, for we find in the twelfth-century *tenson* of Bernart Arnaut d'Armagnac and Lombarda of Toulouse, Bernart's opening pun: "Lombards volgr'eu esser per na Lombarda" ("I would like to be a Lombard for Lombarda").

[Naviglio that succors my flesh]

The Naviglio, oldest canal district of Milano, where Merini still resides. The canals were originally built in 1177–1257 to direct water from the Ticino River along transport routes within the city. At the beginning of the twentieth century, the Naviglio Grande was a working-class district; it is now more fashionable.

[Stay steady burning olive tree]

Barbara is the second of Merini's four daughters; the others are Emanuela (Manuela), Flavia, and Simona. In 1970, at 39, Merini underwent forced sterilization while under psychiatric care.

On the Death of My Sister

Merini's older sister, Anna. She also has a younger brother, Ezio.

The Raven

The "fat body of Ulysses" might refer to any of the numerous sacrifices of sheep made by the epic hero, but perhaps especially to Ulysses' use of lambs to hide his men and a ram to hide himself as they escaped the cave of the wounded Cylops, and their later sacrifice of the animals.

[In the land of Scottland]

This poem was composed for Brunella Antomarini as a gift in September 2001; it is one of many occasional poems, written on the spot or delivered over the telephone, that Merini has made for visitors and friends.

Made in the USA
Las Vegas, NV
13 August 2022

53199137R00083